# KILLER CHILD

# MARY BELL: A TRAGIC TRUE STORY

SYLVIA PERRINI

**TRUE CRIME: BUS STOP READS**

PUBLISHED BY:
GOLDMINEGUIDES.COM
**Copyright © 2015**
Sylviaperrini.goldmineguides.com

All rights reserved.

No part of this publication may be copied, reproduced in any format, by any means, electronic or otherwise, without prior consent from the copyright owner and publisher of this book.

This book is for informational and entertainment purposes. The author or publisher will not be held responsible for the use of any information contained within this eBook.

**DISCLAIMER**

In researching this book, I gathered material from a wide variety of resources, newspapers, academic papers, and other material both on and offline. In many cases, I have referenced actual quotes pertaining to the content throughout. To the best of my knowledge, the material contained is correct. Neither the publisher nor the author will be held liable for incorrect or factual mistakes.

## TABLE OF CONTENTS

| | |
|---|---|
| **MARY BELL** | 1 |
| **MARTIN BROWN** | 10 |
| **BRIAN HOWE** | 23 |
| **INVESTIGATION** | 29 |
| **ARREST** | 42 |
| **THE TRIAL** | 56 |
| **SENTENCING** | 68 |
| **EARLY YEARS** | 73 |
| **THE INCARCERATION OF MARY BELL** | 81 |
| **RELEASE** | 103 |
| **PUBLICATION OF *CRIES UNHEARD*** | 115 |
| **SOURCES** | 120 |
| **OTHER BOOKS BY SYLVIA PERRINI** | 121 |

# MARY BELL

**The child who kills is the child who never had a chance**

Crimes by juveniles (arson, robbery, assault with weapons, manslaughter, murder, and rape) have all increased significantly in the western world over the past few decades. However, one story which sent shock waves through a nation happened as early as 1968 in the northeastern city of Newcastle upon Tyne in England.

Newcastle upon Tyne sits on the north bank of the River Tyne 8.5 miles

(13.7 km) from the North Sea. In the 19th century, shipbuilding, coal mining, and heavy engineering made the city prosper, and it became a powerhouse of the British Industrial Revolution.

However, in the 1960s, Newcastle was a decaying city. The decline of the shipbuilding and mining industries had virtually brought the city to economic ruin. The city, during this period, held the highest crime record, highest unemployment figures, and the highest rate of alcoholism in the whole of the United Kingdom.

## SCOTSWOOD

And nowhere was this poverty so clearly seen than in Scotswood, an impoverished slum area of approximately half a square mile on a hillside, three miles west of the city centre; it was an area that had barely changed since the end of WWII and was an area notorious in the 1960s for its social problems and difficult families that accompany years of deprivation and neglect. With the high unemployment figures, it was common for the men in the area, husbands and fathers, to be drunk. Many of the residents in the area were well known to the police for drunkenness and petty crime. Calls to the police for domestic abuse and fights in the streets were frequent. Here rundown, back-to-back government housing stretched down the hillside to the industrial wasteland on the banks of the River Tyne. The local children played out in the derelict streets and the wasteland, which the children called the "Tin Lizzie," often for hours without parental supervision and without fear of molestation. The "Tin Lizzie" sat next to railway lines and was littered with construction materials, old cars, and dangerous wreckage. Of course, there was the occasional accident and certain areas parents warned their children to stay away from like some of the old derelict houses, in what was known as "rat's alley" which they considered unsafe. Here the children, as a pastime, would throw stones at the windows. However, generally, the parents never considered their children might be at risk.

The majority of the homes in the area didn't have much, just the bare minimum of furniture and a TV. Despite the poverty and problems, it was a close-knit community where almost everybody in the neighborhood knew one another and looked out for one another and each other's children; there was a small local shop, "Dixon's" and the "Woodland's Crescent Nursery" with a sandpit that was another favorite play area with the local children.

On May 11, 1968, John Best, a three-year-old boy, was found at the bottom of an embankment behind some empty sheds near the Delaval Arms public house, bleeding from the head and dazed. He was taken to the public house and claimed that he had been pushed off a ledge but would not say by whom. Even for young children in the area telling the authorities anything was considered bad form. The police and ambulance were called, but the incident was considered accidental and no action was taken.

The following day, seven-year-old Pauline Watson and two friends were playing in the Woodland´s Crescent Nursery sandpit when two local girls, ten-year-old Mary Bell, a cousin of the little boy John Best, and her best friend thirteen-year old-Norma Bell (no relation despite the same surname) joined them. Mary told Pauline to get out of the sandpit and when she refused, Mary put her hands around her neck and squeezed hard, while simultaneously attempted to shove sand down her throat. The other two girls managed to pull Mary off, and Pauline ran home in tears to her mother and reported what had happened. Mary and Norma then scuttled off. Mrs. Watson, despite Pauline's protests as she was terrified what Norma and Mary might do to her, called the police. The police questioned Mary and Norma about the incident, and each girl blamed the other. Norma declared afterwards that Mary was no longer her friend; a declaration that lasted no more than one night. According to the May 15th official police report, both Mary and Norma were warned as to their future conduct.

Mary and Norma lived next door to

each other on Whitehouse Road, one of the roughest streets in the area, and had become best friends since Norma Bell had moved in to the house next to Mary in 1967. Norma, the third of eleven children, lived with her ten brothers and sisters ranging in age from a handicapped brother of sixteen to a small baby of a few months old.

Mary lived with her mother Betty Bell, her stepfather (whom Mary thought at the time was her father) Billy Bell, a drunkard and petty criminal, and her younger half brother and two younger half sisters who she didn't realize were half-siblings. It was a chaotic household.

Her mother was a depressive, erratic, alcoholic who was frequently away working as a prostitute in Glasgow. Betty Bell's specialty was sadomasochism, which the police later believed, although it was never brought up in court, that Mary must have witnessed on a daily basis when her mother was working from home. Betty was later to tell a social worker,

"I always hid the whips from the kids."

# MARTIN BROWN

On Saturday the 25th of May in 1968 blond, shiny, blue-eyed, four-year-old Martin Brown, while his parent's were enjoying a morning lie in, carried up some milk and a Rusk biscuit to his one-year-old sister Linda, whom he shared a bedroom with. It was his normal weekend routine.

Martin lived in a two storey house at 140 St Margaret's Road with his father Georgie and his mother June. His aunt Rita and her five children lived a few doors away on the same street at number 112.

After having given Linda her milk and biscuit, Martin carried the baby into his mother before scuttling down the stairs to eat his own breakfast of "Sugar Pops," his favorite breakfast cereal. Martin then slipped on his anorak before calling upstairs to his mother "I'm away, Mam" and then shot out the door to play with his friends.

That was the last time June Brown heard or saw her young, mischievously faced son alive.

Other people saw him that morning. Two city electricians, Gordan Collinson and John Hall, gave him a biscuit as he watched them work. His Aunt Rita saw him when he called into her house and was fed an egg on toast.

She also saw him again in the afternoon when he dropped by and asked for a piece of bread. His father saw him briefly when he returned home at 3 p.m. to ask for some change to buy a lollypop from Dixon's.

At 3.30 p.m., three teenage boys who were foraging for wood in a derelict house, number 85 St Margaret's Road, found Martin in an upstairs bedroom, flat on his back, his little arms outstretched, and blood and saliva dribbling from his mouth. They called out to the city electricians, still working in the street, for help. Gordan Collinson phoned for an ambulance, and John Hall gave him CPR. Neighbors hearing the commotion ran out of their houses, this included June

Brown and her sister Rita, who arrived at the scene to see John Hall attempting to revive Martin. Martin was transported to Newcastle Hospital and was pronounced dead upon arrival.

The police found no signs of violence, Martin's clothes were undamaged, and there were no broken bones. He had no visible strangulation marks or any other marks. A bottle of aspirin was found in the rubble of the room, which made the police think briefly of possible accidental poisoning, until the toxicity report came back negative. The authorities concluded that Martin's death was accidental, although they had no idea of what caused it. The official report declared the "cause of death open." The residents of the area blamed Martin's death on the dangerous conditions of the derelict houses. The residents organized protests, calling on the authorities to have the derelict buildings demolished rapidly.

On Sunday the 26th of May, Mary Bell, known to friends and neighbors as May, celebrated her eleventh birthday with her friend Norma Bell. During the celebrations, Norma's father saw Mary attempt to throttle his ten-year-old-daughter, Susan, and smacked Mary's hands loose. At the time, Mr. Bell dismissed the incident as over excitement.

A couple of day's following the death of Martin, on hearing a knock at her front door, June Brown, Martin's mother, opened it to find Mary and Norma standing there smiling. Mary asked to see Martin.

June replied, "No, pet. Martin is dead."

"Oh, I know he's dead. I wanted to see him in his coffin," Mary replied grinning.

June, deep in grief, slammed the door on them and their strange request.

Mary and Norma also plagued Martin's Aunt Rita. They would knock on Rita's door and ask her, as they grinned,

"Do you miss Martin?" and "Do you cry for him?"

In the end, Rita, unable to stand it anymore, told them to stop bothering her and to never again call at her house.

The following morning on May the 27th, teachers at the "Woodland's Crescent Nursery," which young Martin Brown had attended, discovered a break in. School supplies had been recklessly strewn about, cleaning materials splattered over the floors, and four disturbing handwritten notes were discovered.

Notes:

"Look out THERE are Murders about"

"I murder so THAT I may come back"

"fuch of we murder watch out Fanny and Faggot"

"we did murder Martain brown F***

of you Bastard"

The police were called and took the notes, which they noted had each letter written alternately in two different handwritings, and filed them away as a sick prank. The nursery school, following the incident, had an alarm system installed.

That same day at the Delaval Road Junior School that Mary and Norma attended, Mary wrote in her school notebook:

*'On Saturday, I was in the house, and my mam sent Me to ask Norma if she Would come up the top with me? we went up and we came down at Magrets Road and there were crowds of people beside an old house. I asked what was the matter. there had been a boy*

*who Just lay down and Died.'*

Next to the story, Mary had drawn a picture of a child in the same position as that in which Martin Brown had been found; close by the body she had drawn a bottle with the word "TABLET" labeled on it. Mary's school notebook story did not strike her teacher, Eric Foster, as strange as it was a momentous event in the small community, although Mary was the only student who wrote about it.

The schoolteachers at Delaval Road Junior School found Mary to be a highly intelligent child but worried occasionally about her seemingly lack of feeling for other people. Mary was a sweet-faced, very pretty child, with a heart-shaped face and pretty blue piecing eyes under a dark heavy fringe. One morning, Eric Foster noticed one of his young girl pupils with what looked like a burn mark on her face. He questioned her about it. The girl said that Mary had snubbed a cigarette out on her cheek. Eric Foster then questioned Mary about it and asked her if she had done it.

"Oh yes," she had replied.

Mr. Foster then asked her if she was sorry about it, and she had replied, "Yes," but without much conviction. Tragically, nothing was done about Mary's violent behavior. Most of the children at the school tried to avoid Norma and Mary on the playground.

Norma was also a pretty girl with dark brown hair and soft brown eyes in a round face. The teachers found her to be slow-witted, with a variety of learning difficulties. The joke among the teachers and others in the neighborhood was that if Mary had asked Norma to jump off the Tyne Bridge she would have done it.

In early June, a twelve-year-old boy, David McCready, witnessed Mary scratch her friend Norma, knock her to the ground, and kick her in the eye in the Nursery sandpit. He later said that Mary screamed,

"I am a murderer!" as she pointed at the house where Martin Brown was found. "That house over there, that's where I killed..."

The boy dismissed the comment as Mary had a reputation among the local kids as being a show-off and a liar.

Early in July, the recently installed alarm went off at the Woodland´s Crescent Nursery. Mary Bell and Norma Bell were caught breaking in, but both denied having broken in before. They were both charged with breaking and entry and a date was set for them to appear at Juvenile Court before being released to the custody of their parents.

Towards the end of July, Mary visited the Howe family, close neighbors, and declared,

"I know something about Norma that will get her put away."

She told them that, "Norma put her hands on a boy's throat. It was Martin Brown -- she pressed and he just dropped."

To illustrate her statement, she clutched her own throat in a choking gesture and then left the house.

# BRIAN HOWE

On the 31st of July in 1968, fourteen-year-old Pat Howe was at home at 64 Whitehouse Road making supper for her younger brothers: seven-year-old Norman and three-year-old Brian. Pat lived in the house with her father, Eric, her two younger brothers, and an older brother Albert. The mother had walked out on the family some eighteen months previously. Pat had taken on the role of surrogate mother, ran the house, and looked after the two younger children with the help of neighbors and friends.

When at 5 p.m. Brian hadn't arrived home for his supper, Pat began to worry and went outside to call him. Down the street outside number 66, Pat saw Mary Bell sitting on the doorstep. She called out,

"Mary, have you seen our Brian?"

"No, but I'll come and help you look for him," Mary offered helpfully.

The two girls set off to look for the three-year-old toddler, and Norma shortly joined them. They first made their way to the local shop "Dixon's", asking along the way if anyone had seen the small boy. They continued searching the streets and neighborhood with Pat becoming progressively more worried. They went up to the railway bridge from where they could get a good view of the industrial wasteland the "Tin Lizzie." From this vantage point, they could see no signs of any children.

"He might be playing behind the blocks or between them," Mary said as she pointed to some large slabs of concrete blocks.

"Oh no, he never goes there," Norma said, who knew Brian well as she sometimes babysat Brian and his best friend John Finlay. Pat agreed with her, as she knew her baby brother didn't like to stray too far from home. The girls had another walk around the streets and popular play areas of the local kids and checked to see if while they had been out he had returned home. At 7p.m., Pat phoned the police and reported Brian missing.

The police began a search. By this time, most of the neighborhood had heard that the toddler was missing and joined in the search party.

The police found Brian Howe shortly after 11 p.m. He was lying between the concrete slabs Mary Bell had pointed at hours earlier. His little body, still dressed, had been covered with grass and purple weeds that grew in abundance over the "Tin Lizzie." Brian had been strangled. There were scratch marks on his nose, blood-stained froth had oozed from his mouth, and his lips were blue. On his neck, there were pressure marks and scratches. Found lying in the grass close to his body were a pair of scissors with one blade bent back and one blade broken.

A murder inquiry was launched. Initially, the police suspected that there was a pervert loose. However, following the autopsy they changed their thinking.

Residents of the area began to wonder if Martin Brown's death was not an accident after all.

During the autopsy on Brian's body, six puncture marks were found on his thighs, and the toddler's genitals had been partially skinned. On his stomach, the letter "M" had been cut into his skin with a razor blade. On closer examination, it looked as if the initial had originally been an "N," but then changed.

He put the time of death down to between 3:30 p.m. to 4:30 p.m. on the 31st of July in 1968.

The pathologist, Mr Bernard Tomlinson, thought that due to the lightness of the pressure marks on Brian's neck and the six puncture wounds indicated that the injuries had been caused by a child or children.

# INVESTIGATION

Police began conducting house-to-house inquiries and interviewing all of the children in the neighborhood. Within 24 hours, over a thousand homes in the area had been visited and 1,200 children between the ages of three to fifteen were interviewed and asked to fill out questionnaires.

The police then examined all the questionnaires and selected twelve children they wanted additional information from; two of the children were Norma Bell and Mary Bell.

Detective Kerr first visited Norma

## INVESTIGATION

Bell's house. Part of the replies on her questionnaire were unreadable, in particular her answer to when she had last seen Brian Howe. Detective Kerr found Norma's behavior strange. He was investigating the murder of a toddler she had known well, and Norma had kept grinning at him as if it was a joke.

Norma made a new statement saying that she had last seen Brian Howe at about 12:45 p.m., on the 31st of July when he was playing with his brother and two little girls on the corner of Whitehouse Road.

Asked what she was doing on the afternoon of July 31st, she stated that between 1-5 p.m., she played in the street with Gillian and Linda Routledge. They then went into the Routledge house at 59 Whitehouse Road and made pom poms.

Detective Kerr then went next door to 70 Whitehouse Road, where Mary Bell lived. However, her stepfather Billy, a big rough gypsy type, at first refused him access to Mary and threatened to set the family Alsatian on him.

If her parents were somehow responsible for young Mary's behavior, she would not talk about it. She had been taught to keep quiet, especially around authority figures. Mary and her younger brothers and sisters were instructed to always call Billy "Uncle," in front of authority figures so that their mother could collect government assistance as a single mother.

## INVESTIGATION

When Detective Kerr was finally allowed access to Mary, he wanted clarification on two questions from her.

1. When had she last seen Brian?
2. Was she playing near the Delaval Arms public house near to the railway lines between 1 p.m. and 5 p.m. on Wednesday the 31st of July?

Mary stated that she had last seen Brian Howe on Whitehouse Road at about 12:30 p.m. playing with his brother. She denied being near the Delaval Arms or the waste ground near there on Wednesday the 31st of July.

Over the next few days, police interviewed Norma and Mary on a number of occasions.

On Friday August the 2nd during an interview, Mary told Detective Sergeant Docherty that she had remembered seeing a boy on his own on Delaval Road after Brian had been killed. He was covered in grass and little purple flowers. She claimed he had scissors in his hands and something was wrong with them "like one leg was either broken or bent. And I saw him trying to cut a cat's tail off with those scissors."

The police interviewed the boy mentioned by Mary, and he had a solid alibi for his whereabouts on the afternoon in question. He had been all afternoon at Newcastle airport, eight miles away, with his parents. He was immediately eliminated from their inquiries.

## INVESTIGATION

At this time, no details of the scissors found lying in the grass close to Brian's body had been photographed or described in any way in the newspapers. By mentioning the scissors, Mary became a prime suspect along with Norma Bell, who had already changed her statement twice. It was becoming clear to the detectives that either Mary, Norma, or both girls had seen Brian die and that one or the other of them was the killer.

Also, the police had several witness statements that Norma and Mary had been seen together that afternoon; yet, neither girl had mentioned this fact in their statements. The police returned to Norma's house, and this time took her to Westgate police station where she was cautioned about her rights and questioned.

Norma now claimed that Mary had told her that she had killed Brian and had taken her to see his body at the blocks. She said that when she saw Brian, she knew he was dead, "because his lips were purple." Norma stated that Mary had said,

"I squeezed his neck and pushed up his lungs; that's how you kill them."

The police detained Norma in a children's home overnight. They then had Mary picked up shortly after midnight and brought to Westgate Road police station accompanied by her Aunt Audrey, as her mother was away working in Glasgow, even though it was late at night and Mary was asleep in bed. Mary, despite three hours of questioning and having been told that Norma had made a statement implicating her in Brian's murder, stuck to her statement although she conceded that she had taken her Alsatian dog to the park for a walk and that Norma had briefly joined her.

The police were astounded by Mary's intelligence and the sophisticated way she second-guessed their questions. Mary would answer the first question before it was even finished and continue answering more questions before they had even been asked.

Detective Dobson, the lead detective in the case, said to Mary,

"I have reason to believe that when

you were near the concrete blocks with Norma, a man shouted at some children who were nearby and you both ran away from where Brian was lying in the grass. This man will probably know you."

"He would have to have good eyesight," Mary replied.

"Why would he need good eyesight?" Detective Dobson asked, thinking he was about to catch the eleven-year-old out in a lie.

"Because he was... "Mary said, and after a pregnant pause added, "clever to see me when I wasn't there."

She refused to make another statement.

"I am making no statements. I have made many statements. It's always me you come for. Norma's a liar; she always tries to get me into trouble."

The police sent Mary home at 3 a.m. having no solid evidence to hold her any longer.

The following day, August 7th, was the day of little Brian Howe's funeral. It was a hot August day. Over two hundred people turned up for the funeral, many of them strangers to the Howe family. Masses of flowers were sent from all around Britain.

Detective Dobson stood outside the Howe's house as the tiny coffin was carried out so, too, was Mary Bell. Detective Dobson later said,

"I was, of course, watching her. And it was when I saw her there that I knew I did not dare risk another day. She stood there laughing. Laughing and rubbing her hands. I thought, *'My God, I've got to bring her in, she'll do another one.'*"

Norma, also in the morning, made a fourth statement claiming to have been with Mary earlier and had gone with Mary and Brian to the concrete blocks on the Tin Lizzie. Brian had with him a pair of scissors given to him by his brother. At first, they had all climbed inside an old tank but immediately all climbed out because it was smelly. Norma said it was shortly after that Mary told Brian to lift his neck. Norma continued: She got him down on the grass, and she seemed to go all funny. You could tell there was something the matter with her. She kept on struggling with him, and he was struggling and trying to get her hands away. She let go of him, and I could hear him gasping. She squeezed his neck again, and I said,

"Mary, leave the baby alone," but she wouldn't.

She said to me, "My hands are getting thick; take over."

Then I ran away. I went back the way we had come. Norma claimed she had then gone back to Whitehouse road and played with some other children. Then Mary arrived back twenty minutes later and asked Norma to revisit the scene of the murder. This Norma did and said this time Mary had a razor blade with her which is when she cut the initial 'M' on Brian's tummy. Norma said Mary had then hidden the razor blade.

Norma said they again revisited the murder scene at about 5.30 p.m. This time Norma said Mary cut off lumps of Brian's hair and stabbed his legs with the scissors. Norma, accompanied by police officers, revisited the crime scene and showed them where Mary had hidden the razor blade. This blade was then taken into evidence.

# ARREST

Later that afternoon, Mary was again picked up from home and taken to the police station. This time, Mary appeared nervous and not quite so sure of herself. She made a new and full statement. The following is Mary Bell's official statement:

*I, Mary Flora Bell, wish to make a statement. I want someone to write down what I have to say. I have been told that I need not say anything unless I wish to do so but that whatever I say may be given in evidence.*

*Signed, Mary F. Bell*

*Brian was in his front street and I and Norma were walking along towards him. We walked past him and Norma says,*

*"Are you coming to the shop Brian?"*

*and I says, "Norma, you've got no money, how can you go to the shop? Where are you getting it from?"*

*She says, "Nebby" (keep your nose clean).*

*Little Brian followed and Norma says,*

*"Walk up in front."*

*I wanted Brian to go home, but Norma kept coughing so Brian wouldn't hear us.*

*We went down Crosshill Road with Brian still in front of us. There was this colored boy, and Norma tried to start a fight with him. She said,*

*"Darkie, whitewash, it's time you got washed."*

*The big brother came out and hit her.*

*She shouted,*

*"Howay, put your dukes up."*

*The lad walked away and looked at her as though she was daft.*

*We went beside Dixon's shop and climbed over the railings, I mean, through a hole and over the railway. Then I said,*

*"Norma, where are you going?"*

*and Norma said, "Do you know that little pool where the tadpoles are?"*

*When we got there, there was a big, long tank with a big, round hole with little holes around it. Norma says to Brian,*

*"Are you coming in here because there's a lady coming on the Number 82, and she's got boxes of sweets and that."*

*We all got inside; then, Brian started to cry, and Norma asked him if he had a sore throat. She started to squeeze his throat, and he started to cry. She said,*

*"This isn't where the lady comes; it's over there, by them big blocks."*

*We went over to the blocks and she says,*

*"Ar--you'll have to lie down"*

*and he lay down beside the blocks where he was found. Norma says,*

*"Put your neck up."*

*And he did. Then she got hold of his neck and said,*

*"Put it down."*

*She started to feel up and down his neck. She squeezed it hard. You could tell it was hard because her finger tips were going white. Brian was struggling, and I was pulling her shoulders, but she went mad. I was pulling her chin up but she screamed at me.*

*By this time, she had banged Brian's head on some wood or corner of wood, and Brian was lying senseless. His face was all white and bluey, and his eyes were open. His lips were purplish and had all like slaver on, it turned into something like fluff. Norma covered him up, and I said,*

*"Norma, I've got nothing to do with this. I should tell on you, but I'll not."*

*Little Lassie was there, and it was crying, and she said,*

*"Don't you start or I'll do the same to you."*

*It still cried, and she went to get hold of its throat, but it growled at her. She said,*

*"Now now. Don't be hasty."*

*We went home, and I took little Lassie (Brian's dog) home an all. Norma was acting kind of funny and making twitchy faces and spreading her fingers out. She said,*

*"This is the first, but it'll not be the last."*

*I was frightened then. I carried Lassie and put her down over the railway, and we went up Crosswood Road way. Norma went into the house, and she got a pair of scissors, and she put them down her pants. She says,*

*"Go and get a pen."*

*I said "No. What for?"*

*She says, "To write a note on his stomach."*

*And I wouldn't get the pen. She had a Gillette razor blade. It had Gillette on. We went back to the blocks, and Norma cut his hair. She tried to cut his leg and his ear with the blade. She tried to show me it was sharp. She took the top of her dress where it was raggie and cut it; it made a slit. A man came down the railway bank with a little girl with long blonde hair. He had a red checked shirt on and blue denim jeans. I walked away. She hid the razor blade under a big, square concrete block. She left the scissors beside him. She got out before me over the grass on to Scotswood Road. I couldn't run on the grass cos I just had my black slippers on. When we got along a bit she says,*

*"Mary, you shouldn't have done that cos you'll get into trouble,"*

*And I hadn't done nothing. I haven't got the guts. I couldn't kill a bird by the neck or throat or anything. It's horrible, that. We went up the steps and went home. I was nearly crying. I said,*

*"If Pat finds out, she'll kill you. Never mind killing Brian cos Pat's more like a tomboy. She's always climbing in the old buildings and that."*

*Later on, I was helping to look for Brian, and I was trying to let on to Pat that I knew where he was on the blocks, but Norma said,*

*"He'll not be over there; he never goes ther," and she convinced Pat he wasn't there.*

*I got shouted in about half past seven, and I stayed in. I got woke up about half past eleven, and we stood at the door as Brian had been found: The other day, Norma wanted to get put in a home. She says will you run away with us, and I said no. She says if you get put in a home and you feed the little ones and murder them then run away again.*

*I have read the above statement, and I have been told that I can correct, alter or add anything I wish, this statement is true. I have made it of my own free will.*

*Mary Flora Bell (signed at 6:55 pm)*

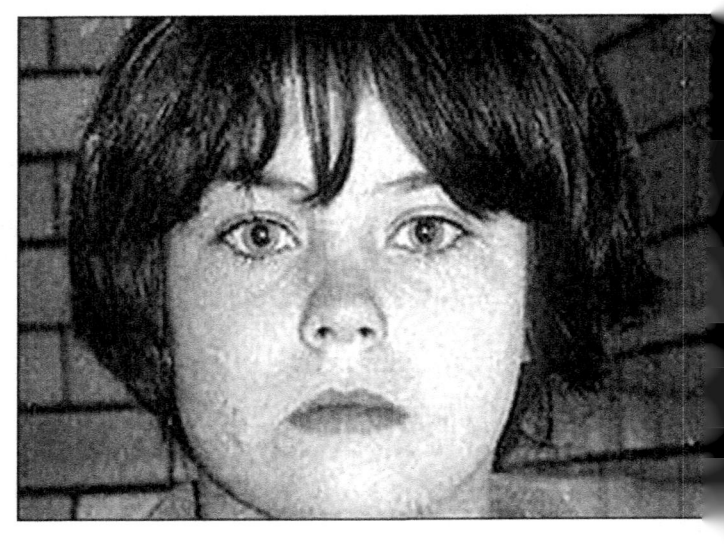

Mary Bell at the time of her arrest

On the 8th of August, the Police

formally charged Norma Bell and Mary Bell with the murder of Brian Howe. Both girls were detained in custody in small jail cells at the police station.

As news of the arrests of the eleven-year-old and thirteen-year-old girls hit the papers, it electrified the country.

Despite Mary's denials, the evidence against Mary was beginning to stack up. The police, by this time, had reopened Martin Brown's case file, as there were many similarities between his death and that of Brian Howe's, and they were now treating it as murder.

Eric Foster, Mary's teacher at Delaval Road Junior School on hearing of Mary's arrest, re-read her school notebooks and handed them into the police. The police were particularly interested in her news-story drawing about Martin Brown's death. The tablets next to Martin's body had never been disclosed to anyone. To the police, it was evidence that Mary had been at the scene of Martin's death.

The first night in their tiny prison cells in the police station, Norma and Mary were restless. They continually shouted to each other through the doors. Mary, who had always been a chronic bed wetter, was petrified of going to sleep, afraid that she might wet her bed. Whenever she did so at home, her mother Betty would severely humiliate her by rubbing her face in the pool of urine and would then hang the mattress outside for the entire neighborhood to see. She was petrified of what punishment she would receive in police custody; she was only an eleven-year-old-child.

Mary, between her arrest and trial, was first sent to an assessment center near London and then to Seaham Remand Home closer to home in County Durham, which catered for girls aged between fourteen and eighteen and was run by the prison department.

Many of the people who cared for Mary in the lead up to the trial became fond of the vivacious, intelligent, little girl that was in such deep trouble. They believed that Mary had no idea of the enormity of what she had done. She fretted about whether her mother would have to pay a fine and hoped her mother wouldn't be 'too upset'. Betty Bell did not visit her daughter for over a week after her arrest and then only to yell at her for the shame she had brought upon her. Mary told a police officer that Brian Howe didn't have a mother, so he wouldn't be missed. At some point one, of her guards asked whether she knew how it would feel to be strangled. Mary replied,

"Why? If you're dead, you're dead. It doesn't matter then."

During her trial Mary told one policewoman,

"Murder isn't that bad. We all die sometime anyway."

Norma, thanks to her barrister, R. P.

Smith, QC, within days of her arrest had persuaded a judge in chambers in London that she should spend the period before the trial as a patient at a nearby mental hospital, the Prudhoe Monkton, being "observed" by nurses and doctors.

# THE TRIAL

The trial of Regina v. Mary Flora Bell and Norma Joyce Bell for the murders of Martin Brown and Brian Howe began on December 5th, 1968 at the Newcastle Assizes in Court Two in front of Judge, Mr. Justice Cusack. It was a trial that fascinated, and at the same time horrified, a nation. Many people felt that the Crown Court was the wrong place to deal with such young children but in England the age of criminal responsibility is ten and so Mary and Norma were tried as adults.

However, to make it less

intimidating for the girls, the Judge ruled that their lawyers could sit with them.

The Prosecutor Mr. Rudolph Lyons began the trial by indicating that whoever murdered Brian Howe also killed Martin Brown. He told the court that the two young girls had murdered "solely for the pleasure and excitement of killing." Rudolf Lyons then proceeded to methodically recount the suspicious behavior of Mary and Norma; how they had harassed the mourning family with their gruesome questions, and Mary's and Norma's smiling and asking if she could see little Martin Brown in his coffin, and how they maliciously vandalized the Woodlands Nursery leaving notes that amounted to a confession.

Handwriting experts were called into the court who said that the notes were written in both girls' handwriting. Forensic pathologists testified that gray fibers from one of Mary's dresses were found on the bodies of both Martin and Brian and that fibers from one of Norma's skirts were discovered on Brian's shoes. Altogether, the prosecution produced thirty-nine witnesses.

Taken all together, the prosecution had a strong case against both Norma and Mary. Both girls pleaded not guilty and blamed each other for the murders.

The two girls were scrutinized heavily by the public and media in court. Norma looked like a terrified frightened little girl, totally overawed by the court proceedings, and frequently breaking into tears. Behind her in the courtroom, she was surrounded by a solid protective loving family, who would frequently comfort her.

Mary, in contrast, showed no emotion and appeared defiant. And although her step-father, mother, aunts, and uncles sat behind her, never did they touch or demonstrate any physical comfort towards her. Mary, unlike Norma, appeared very alone. Mary's mother Betty did not help her case. She frequently disrupted the court proceedings with dramatic sobbing and wailing as her long blond wig would slide off her head, revealing her dark brown hair. On some occasions, she

## THE TRIAL

stormed out of the courtroom clumping on high heels during the trial and then would dramatically reappear just minutes later. Her stepfather Billy sat quietly, head in hand, and ignored his wife's theatrics.

Though highly intelligent, Mary admitted later that she was bewildered by the proceedings. She had little understanding of what was happening to her. She was ignorant of knowing what a jury or a verdict was or what was meant by rules of evidence. No one had attempted to explain to the small girl the alien language and rituals of a trial.

Norma elicited compassion, while Mary only seemed to attract animosity. On the fourth day of the trial, Norma was called to the witness stand. Here, she frequently broke down crying and answered questions in stuttering whispers and gave the impression of a very insecure, emotionally fragile, frightened little girl. The judge was gentle with her and rather protective, giving her frequent breaks if he thought the cross examination was getting too much for her. Everything she blamed on Mary: the strangling, the razor blade initial, the stabbing with the scissors, and the mutilation of Brian's penis. She projected herself as innocent who had the misfortune of having an evil friend. The only thing she could not entirely blame on Mary was the notes written in both girls' handwriting.

## THE TRIAL

A psychiatrist, Dr. Frazer, who had treated Norma at the Prudhoe Monkton Mental Hospital, described Norma as emotionally immature and of sub-normal intelligence, who did not have the capacity "to be a leader." He said that while at the hospital, intelligence tests showed she had the mental age of a child of eight or nine and during her time at the hospital had got on well with the other children and had shown no signs of physical aggression.

On the sixth day of the trial, Mary was called to the witness box. In complete contrast to Norma, she showed no fear or discomfiture but appeared assuredly self-confident as she bandied words and witty quips with the prosecutor, Mr. Rudolph

Lyons.

Spectators in the courtroom watched Mary with horrified curiosity. For a child who was to be branded as manipulative and cunning, she appeared to know little about attracting sympathy.

After Mary's testimony, the defense lawyers called the psychiatrist, Dr. Robert Orton, who had examined Mary. He testified,

"I think that this girl must be regarded as suffering from psychopathic personality," demonstrated by "a lack of feeling quality to other humans," and "a liability to act on impulse and without forethought." And, "She showed no remorse whatsoever, no tears, and no anxiety. She was completely unemotional about the whole affair and merely resentful at her detention."

A Home Office psychiatrist, Dr. Westbury, said that Mary showed no evidence "of mental illness or severe abnormality or sub normality of intelligence," but had a "serious disorder of personality... which required medical treatment." He continued, "Manipulation of people is [her] primary aim."

On cross-examination by Norma's lawyer, Mr. Smith, Dr. Westbury agreed that Mary was "violent" and "very dangerous."

The following day the closing arguments began. The prosecutor, Mr. Rudolph Lyons, branded Mary as a fiend. He said that Norma was a victim of

"...an evil and compelling influence almost like that of the fictional *Svengali*" and continued by saying, "In Norma, you have a simple backward girl of subnormal intelligence. In Mary you have a most abnormal child, aggressive, vicious, cruel, and incapable of remorse; a girl moreover possessed of a dominating personality, with a somewhat unusual intelligence, and a degree of cunning that is almost terrifying."

Norma's lawyer, Mr.Smith, said in his closing speech that Norma had been "an innocent bystander" who had told childish lies to get herself out of trouble.

In an attempt to rescue Mary from being cast off as a devilish "bad seed," Mary's barrister asked broader questions:

Why did this happen? What made Mary do it? Mr. Harvey Robson declared,

"It is... very easy to revile a little girl, to liken her to Svengali without pausing for a moment to ponder how the whole sorry situation has come about..."

On the night of December 16th, eleven-year-old Mary knew that the following day the jury would decide her fate. She said to the policewoman guarding her,

"What would be the worst that could happen to me? Would they hang me?"

The jury, which consisted of five women and seven men, took less than four hours to return a verdict. Mary Bell was found "guilty of Manslaughter in

Martin Brown's and Brian Howe's murders because of Diminished Responsibility."

Norma Bell was acquitted, as she was deemed by the jury as a passive slow-witted partner who had been led astray by the evil and devious Mary Bell.

Mary broke down and cried as she heard the jury's verdicts. Sitting on the benches behind her, her relatives also wept. However, it was only her young solicitor, David Bryson, who put a comforting arm around Mary.

# SENTENCING

In Judge Justice Cusack sentencing he said,

"It is a most unhappy thing that in all the resources of this country it appears there is no hospital available which is suitable for the accommodation of this girl."

He continued, "It is an appalling thing that with a child as young as this one, one has to take into consideration such matters. I am not entirely unsympathetic but anxious, as I am to do everything for her benefit; my primary duty is to protect other people."

"There is a very grave risk to other children if she is not closely watched and every conceivable step taken to see that she doesn't do again what she has been found guilty of. In the case of a child of this age, no question of imprisonment arises. I have power to order a sentence of detention, and it seems to me that no other method of dealing with her in the circumstances is suitable."

"I, therefore, have to turn to what length of detention should be imposed. I say at once that if an undeterminate period is imposed, as in the case of a life sentence of imprisonment, that does not mean that the person concerned is kept in custody indefinitely or for the rest of their natural lives. It means that the position can be considered from time to time and, if it becomes safe to release that person, that person can be released. For that reason, the sentence of the court concurrently in respect of these two matters upon Mary Bell is a sentence of detention and the detention will be for life."

Norma Bell, for breaking and entering the Woodlands Crescent Nursery, was later given three years probation and placed under psychiatric care.

During all of Mary Bell's months in remand and during the trial no one had thought, or even seemed to care, what had made this extraordinarily pretty, blue-eyed, heart-shaped face girl commit these crimes. To the media and the British public, she was seen as a sweet-faced, chilling monster; a freak of nature, simply pure evil. She was described in the press under lurid headlines as a child who had been "born evil," a "demon," and "monster."

The detectives who had arrested Mary didn't see her in this light. They felt sorry for her and felt, given her upbringing, she had never stood a chance of being a normal child. The authorities in their dogged concern with determining Mary's guilt or innocence did not attempt to discover the truth about her horrendous home life.

Perhaps, if the whole truth of Mary's upbringing had been known, then the outcome of the trial may have been very different. Mary was a victim of abuse, appalling abuse that was not uncovered for many years.

# EARLY YEARS

Betty Bell (née McCrickett), was born in 1940, in Glasgow. Betty's mother described her as a profoundly religious child who she thought would grow up to be a nun. Her sister said she was always drawing nuns, altars, graves, and cemeteries.

Betty Bell gave birth to Mary when she was seventeen-years-old on May 26th, 1957 in Gateshead, a large urban town that sits on the south bank of the River Tyne opposite Newcastle upon Tyne.

It is unknown who Mary's

biological father was. The first thing Betty said when Mary was placed into her arms by her mother shortly after giving birth was,

"Take the thing away from me!"

She rejected her daughter and frequently tried to kill her.

It is in Gitta Sereny's book *The Case of Mary Bell*, first published in 1972, where one learns about Mary's early years. Mary's maternal grandmother, uncles, Aunt Isa, and Aunt Cathy co-operated with Ms. Sereny in the hope that the public knowing about Mary's early life, might make them more sympathetic to Mary and show that she was a damaged traumatized little girl and not an evil monster. As told to Ms. Sereny by

Mary's relatives and friends, Mary's childhood was a nightmare of abandonment and drug overdoses.

A few months after Mary was born, Betty met Billy Bell and married him in March of 1958. A few months later in the autumn of 1958, Betty gave birth to Billy's son. At the time, they were living with Betty's mother and sister Isa in Gateshead.

When Mary was aged one she somehow managed to get hold of her grandmother's medication, which she kept hidden inside a gramophone that was placed high up on a chest of drawers. Despite the pills being in a bottle with a childproof cap, Mary succeeded in swallowing enough of the pills to almost kill her. Luckily, her grandmother found her and rushed her to hospital where she had her stomach pumped. Her grandmother suspected Betty of giving Mary the pills.

Shortly afterwards, Betty, Billy, and the two children moved out. In November of 1959, Betty wrote to her sister Cathy and said she had given Mary away to some family friends. Cathy immediately went to visit the friends and returned Mary to Betty. A few months later, Cathy went to visit her sister and took a packet each of sweets for Mary and her younger brother. Leaving the children munching their sweets in the living room, Mary and Cathy went to make a pot of tea in the kitchen. When Cathy returned to the living room, she was horrified to see mixed up with the sweets little triangular blue pills which she recognized as Betty's Drinamyl, amphetamines known as purple hearts. Cathy, before taking the children to hospital, made them drink hot water and salt making both children vomit in the sink, an act that may have saved their lives.

"They must have taken the bottle out of my handbag," was Betty's explanation, which her sister found hard to believe.

When Cathy returned home and told her husband Jack about the incident, he suggested that for Mary's safety they should offer her a home. Cathy wrote to Betty making her the offer, but Betty refused to give Mary up.

A few months later when Betty and Mary were visiting her mother, Betty held Mary up by the open window of the third floor kitchen sink for a pee (the bathroom was on the ground floor). Suddenly Betty's brother, Philip, saw Mary begin to fall out of the window; he leapt up and only just managed to prevent her plunging out the window. The family was getting extremely worried about Mary's safety.

A few days later Betty, secretly followed by Isa, took Mary to an adoption agency and handed her over to a distraught woman who was not allowed to adopt because of her age and other reasons.

"I brought this one in to be adopted. You have her," Betty said, shoving Mary into the stranger's arms.

Isa followed the woman and Mary and, noting down the address, handed it over to her mother. Mary was eventually returned home with new dresses the stranger had bought her.

Mary's next overdose was just a few months later when Mary took a load of "iron pills," apparently mistaking them for Smarties. She had collapsed unconscious and had been rushed to the hospital where she had her stomach pumped. Mary told doctors that her mother had given her the smarties; a fact that was corroborated by a friend of Mary's to her Aunt Cathy. For a developing child, overdoses can cause serious brain damage, a frequent trait amongst violent offenders.

After this incident, furious arguments occurred between Betty, her mother, and siblings which culminated in Betty telling them she never wanted to see them again, and she cut off all contact with them for over a year.

As if these abuses weren't bad enough, the real horror of Mary Bell's childhood was not to surface until many years after her release from prison.

# THE INCARCERATION OF MARY BELL

As Mary Bell's case was unique, the United Kingdom, who had never before been presented with an eleven-year-old murderess, was unsure what to do with her. Prison was not an option for a child. The Mental health hospitals weren't equipped to take her, and she was considered too dangerous for facilities that housed troubled children.

Straight after sentencing and after a brief visit by her relatives, the terrified

## INCARCERATION

Mary had a blanket thrown over her head and was led out of court blinded. Mary thought she was being taken to the gallows but was taken to Low Newton, an adult prison, in County Durham. Here, she was stripped, searched, and hosed down in the same manner as adult prisoners. As there was no prison uniform small enough, she was allowed to wear her own clothes. She was then put in isolation in the hospital wing of the prison. As it was law that she must receive education whilst incarcerated due to her age, the woman governor of the prison spent an hour a day with Mary reading and writing. Mary liked the governor and mentioned her fear of being hanged. The governor assured her that no one was going to hang her.

While Mary was incarcerated in Low Newton, her mother and step-father were trying to sell her story to the tabloid press. For once, the tabloid press was sickened by such a mercenary act on the part of her parents that they refused to touch the story.

Mary spent about two weeks at Low Newton before being transferred, shortly before Christmas, to Cumberlow Lodge: a high-security, short-term remand home for girls aged fifteen to seventeen, while the government frantically searched for a solution as to where to house the eleven-year-old Mary, long-term.

In February of 1969, Mary was

taken to Red Bank reform schools Special Unit in Lancashire. It was a school for boys, and Mary was the only girl among twenty-two boys in the special unit for nearly all the five years she was there. It wasn't ideal but was the best the government could come up with. Mr. Dixon, who ran the school, travelled down to London to pick Mary up with his wife. Mary immediately took a liking to James Dixon and over time came to love and respect him. He was an ex-Navy man known for his strong moral character. To Mary, he became a strong, benevolent, father figure who provided structure and discipline for Mary that had been so lacking in her life.

The special unit sat in the middle of

the reform school, which catered for around 500 boys. The children in the special unit were not free to mix with the children in the reform school as they were children who required a high-degree of security and who were kept locked in at all times. Despite this, it was, according to Gitta Sereny, who visited the unit a few times, a pleasant environment. It was light and modern. On the ground floor, there was a library, sitting rooms with comfortable chairs, a pleasant dining room, and a number of classrooms where the children were taught in small groups, depending on age and ability. Outside was a garden, a greenhouse, and a shed for pets. The children in the special unit also had the use of the swimming pool in the main reform school for an hour a day in the summer and access to the extensive sports facilities.

Upstairs, were the dormitories. When it was decided Mary was to be sent to the special unit, an area had been sectioned off for girls. However, during the entire time Mary was there, only five other girls were housed there and only for short amounts of time, the longest being three months.

The schedule at Redbank was regimented. The children were to be up at 7 a.m sharp, then shower, make their beds, and be downstairs for fingernail and shoe inspection before breakfast at 8 a.m. Lessons were from 8 a.m. to 12:45. Lunch was served promptly at 1 p.m.

followed by more lessons between 2 p.m. to 4 p.m. Between 4-5 p.m., they could choose to play draughts or chess. The last cooked meal of the day was at 5 p.m. In the summer, they then had swimming at 6 p.m., followed by athletics or football. At 8 p.m. they had showers and then hot cocoa and a sandwich. Occasionally, they would be allowed to watch television if something suitable was deemed to be on. Bedtime was from 8:30 to 9 p.m. and lights out was at 9:30 p.m. There was a house-mother, Miss Hemmings, who looked over the children, and who grew to adore Mary.

The philosophy of Red Bank was to focus on the present. James Dixon believed that dwelling on the past was detrimental. He was of the belief that love and proper care could conquer all. A visiting psychiatrist to Redbank, Dr Dewi Jones, disagreed. He thought Mary was blocking out her troubled past and was being discouraged from attempting to discover why she had killed the two little boys. He put in a request to treat Mary individually at Redbank and was granted permission to see her once a week for between 30-60 minutes. He realized rapidly that for a child as severely disturbed as Mary, it was an inadequate amount of time to give her the attention he believed she needed. He requested that she be brought to him two to three times a week at the local hospital psychiatric unit. His request was turned down, leaving Mary to continue denying her crimes and the reasons for them.

The first ten months that Mary was at Redbank her stepfather, Billy Bell, whom Mary loved, visited regularly. Mary, who was never allowed to be alone with visitors, would sit and chat in one of the sitting rooms accompanied by one of the Redbank staff. Mary looked forward to and enjoyed his visits and news of her young siblings whom she missed. During one of the visits, Billy told her that her mother had left home for good, and they were to divorce. Billy's visits came to an abrupt halt when he was arrested and imprisoned for robbery with assault. Billy's sister, Aubrey, took in Mary's three young siblings, as Betty had no contact with them and had abandoned them. Betty had taken up with a new man, George, ten years her junior.

Betty Bell first visited Mary at Redbank in December of 1969 and continued visiting once or twice a month until April of 1970. The staff noted that after each of Betty's visits, Mary would become unsettled, difficult to deal with, and aggressive towards the other children. Betty used her visits to Mary to sell tidbits of information of Mary's life to the tabloid press. Betty enjoyed making Mary feel guilty as to how much she suffered as the mother of an infamous child murderer.

"Jesus was only nailed to the cross, I'm being hammered," Betty would complain to Mary.

James Dixon pondered about stopping Betty's visits to Mary but in that era, to prevent a mother's access to her daughter was unthinkable. In the end, Mary herself asked James Dixon to stop allowing her mother to visit.

However, the visits by Betty began again in the spring of 1971.

In the spring of 1970, Mary told her female counselor that a housemaster on night duty had sexually assaulted her. She asked the counselor not to tell anyone but, as it was the counselor's job, she did. Mary was questioned about the incident, but her evidence was considered unreliable. However, from that point on, Mr. Dixon insisted that all night duties were to be carried out in pairs.

Of course, today we are all aware, far too frequently, of reading in the press about children being assaulted in the care of foster homes, of monsters, such as Sir Jimmy Saville, getting away for decades with sexually abusing children in hospitals and elsewhere, and none believing the children who were abused. Society was not geared to hear such unacceptable truths from a child at the expense of an adult, especially a child such as Mary Bell.

In July of 1971, the home office psychiatrist, Dr Westbury, visited Mary. At the trial, he had testified that Mary had a "serious disorder of personality," and that "Manipulation of people is [her] primary aim," and that she was "violent" and "very dangerous."

In his report to the home office after visiting Mary at Redbank, Dr. Westbury said he had "found her remarkably improved," and had lost "nearly all of her aggressive tendencies." He suggested that a release date when Mary was 18 in 1975 should be considered.

In 1973, Mary, aged 16, sat her O'Levels examinations. She passed them all. She and Mr. Dixon were hoping that she might be able to be moved to the reform school soon, still supervised by James Dixon, and be allowed out daily to take her 'A' Levels in the local college and then go on to university. Mary was beginning to see a future for herself far removed from her abusive deprived childhood.

This dream was shattered when she was informed in November of 1973, by an extremely disappointed and saddened Mr. Dixon, that she was to be moved to prison. Mary was stunned. Her years at Redbank had been relatively happy and secure. It had become her home. She had progressed greatly in her time there from the damaged child she had been when she had first arrived. Mr. Dixon said he had done everything he could to make the Home Office change its mind but to no avail. It was a traumatic decision, not just for Mary, but for the staff at Redbank as well, in particular Mr. Dixon, who felt he had let Mary down.

The following day, Mr. and Mrs. Dixon drove the terrified sixteen-year-old Mary to Styal Women's prison in Cheshire, a large oppressive Redbrick Victorian building, in which she would be the youngest inmate.

Gitta Sereny wrote in her book *Cries Unheard*,

"There can be little doubt that this transfer was destructive for Mary."

Mary had to adjust from a caring almost entirely male community at Red Bank to a full women's adult prison. She became rebellious and was frequently punished. Mary, as part of her rebellion, decided to go "butch." When Betty Bell heard this, she said,

"Jesus Christ, what next? You're a

murderer and now you're a lesbian?"

While in Styal, Mary learned that Billy Bell was not her biological father. This created in her an acute identity crisis. She wondered just who was she? The next time her mother visited her, she asked her who her biological father was. Her mother refused to answer and abruptly ended the visit.

In June of 1977, Mary was transferred to an open prison, Moor Court in Staffordshire, a beautiful 17th century manor house with pleasant gardens set in the countryside. Mary, having been locked up for the last ten years of her life in institutionalized buildings, found it hard to deal with, especially as she had still not been given any kind of release date. Within three months, along with another girl, Annette Priest, a 21-year-old prostitute and thief, she escaped.

Two young men who were on their way to Blackpool, a holiday resort on the North-East English coast which is famous for its funfair, picked up the two girls. Mary, now aged 20, had never seen the sea nor had she been to a funfair, nor had she ever been to a nightclub or drank alcohol, and had never had vaginal sex. In the two days she was free, she experienced all of these things before the young man she was with turned her over to the authorities and later sold his story to the tabloids.

Once back in police custody, Mary

was taken to Risley prison in Cheshire, known among prisoners as Grisly Risley due to its 'barbarous, squalid, dirty, and dilapidated conditions.' Mary remained here for three months before being sent back to Styal. After nine months back in Styal, she was informed in September that she was to be released in May of the following year.

Mary was then moved to another open prison, Askham Grange, near York. Askham Grange was built in 1886 as a country house and although now a prison, it still retains a country-house feel to it. The brickwork is mellow and the grounds immaculate. At Askham Grange an outside visitor, a student from York University, introduced Mary to the music and youth culture of the times. She was also visited weekly by a psychiatrist who, like Mary, became increasingly concerned about her abilities to readjust to the outside world.

After three months, she was moved to a hostel in the grounds of Askham House and was given employment in a local restaurant as a waitress and then in a factory in Leeds, assembling electrical equipment. To get there, she had a mile-long walk to the bus stop and then two bus journeys. She felt "anxious and shaky" in public and would often find comfort in the ladies' lavatory because she was "behind a locked door" again. Her constant fear was that she would be recognized and within two weeks Mary's fears were realized: the tabloid press had discovered her movements, possibly from Betty Bell, and published details with photographs of her. Mary, when informed by the prison, was deeply upset. She kept asking, "Why can't they leave me alone?"

While at Askham, she met a local married man who fell in love with her. On her first home leave, she went and stayed with her mother and her new husband George. Her mother plied her with drink and introduced her to her new friends as her cousin. She forbade Mary to tell anyone she was her daughter. The experience left her utterly confused. In the morning at her mother's house, she had gotten up and stacked the sheets on her bed as she had done in prison for twelve years. Mary has since admitted that it took her years to rid herself of routine prison habits.

On returning to Askham, Mary soon discovered she was pregnant by the married man who had been, according to Mary, determined to show her she wasn't a lesbian. She was in a terrible dilemma. She did not know what to do. On the one hand, she wanted to keep the baby but was unsure if she would be able to look after herself, let alone a baby, and in all likelihood the baby would be removed from her care. She talked to the probation officers at the hostal and feeling she had no choice had an abortion. She later said to the author Gitta Sereny,

"But if I think that almost the first thing I did after twelve years in prison for killing two babes was to kill the baby in me...." before breaking down in tears.

Prior to Mary's release from prison, she needed to be given a new identity in order for her to have a chance at leading a normal life without the press or the hating public hounding her. This was because she was a high-profile case, partly due to her mother constantly feeding news about Mary to the tabloids, and because of her horrific crimes.

Mary, on learning of her new identity, wondered how she would cope with pretending to be someone other than Mary.

# RELEASE

Mary Bell was released May 14, 1980, at the age of 23. She spent her first night of freedom in the isolated rural home of her probation officer in Suffolk on the east coast of England where she laid low for two weeks. During this time, Mary was plagued by anxiety, sleeplessness, indecision, found everything "strange and alien," and missed the security of prison.

From Suffolk, she went and lived with a family in Yorkshire. Here, she found herself a job in a nursery school, but her probation officer said it was not appropriate for her to be working with children. She then took a series of jobs, mostly waitressing. She enjoyed living with the family but then at Christmas her mother Betty turned up with her husband George. Betty persuaded Mary to return home with them to Whitley Bay, a seaside town on the North Sea coast in North Tyneside. Mary, after two weeks with her mother, who was constantly drunk, moved out and went to live in York. Here, she enrolled into a college and studied psychology, philosophy, and English Literature. She began to harbor dreams of becoming a teacher or therapist, until her probation officer dashed her aspirations by telling her that because of her past crimes those careers were prohibited professions for her. Depressed, she dropped out of college and once again returned to her mother and George.

While staying with her mother, she met a young man who was several years younger than herself. He became her first proper boyfriend. After constant roughs with her mother, she finally moved in with him.

The young couple got married, and Mary gave birth to their daughter on May 25 1984 ironically, 16 years to the day she had killed Martin Brown.

Officials were greatly concerned over whether Mary, having murdered two children, should be allowed to keep her child, but Mary fought hard for the right to keep her daughter. The child was made a ward of court, but Mary was allowed to bring her up. News of the birth was leaked to the media, possibly by Betty Bell, but a High Court injunction protected the child from being identified until the age of eighteen.

All was well until a couple of years into the marriage. Her young husband started going out more and more and discussing Mary with his friends. He was also on occasion violent towards Mary. By May of 1988, the marriage was over.

Betty's marriage to George also ended. George told Mary he just couldn't handle Betty anymore but would always remain Mary's friend.

Mary then met a new partner, X,

and they moved with her small daughter to a small village. Mary constantly lived in fear of being exposed and when the villagers discovered Mary's identity, they marched through the village street with "Murderer Out!" signs. The small family decided to relocate to a seaside town in the south of England. Here they lived happily, undisturbed for a number of years. They kept their address hidden from Betty whom Mary believed, with good reason, had leaked her address and whereabouts to the press before. Mary had not seen her mother for several years but invited her to spend two days with them over Christmas in 1994.

Ever since Mary had discovered that Billy Bell was not her real father, she had been tortured by the question of whom her real father was. She suspected that Betty's father, Mary's grandfather, had abused her mother and that she may have been the result of this abuse. When staying with her mother, she looked through a large scrapbook her mother kept and discovered love poems Betty had written to her father. Later in life, she asked her mother directly if this was the case.

Her mother replied quietly, "You are the devil's spawn," and refused to say more.

Her mother died at the beginning of January in 1995. The post mortem and inquest concluded that she had died of pneumonia.

Following Betty Bell's death, Gitta Sereny approached Mary about the idea of writing a book about her life. By this time, several foreign and British publications had over the years since her release approached Mary and offered her huge sums of money for her story, all of which she had turned down. Up to this point, the only one who had profited from Mary's story was Betty Bell, who had never given a penny to Mary. Moreover, as one was to learn from *Cries Unheard*, Betty prostituted Mary in every conceivable way.

Mary agreed to meet Gitta Sereny and eventually agreed to co-operate with her in the writing of *Cries Unheard*. Gitta Sereny felt that as the book would involve months of hard work on Mary's part, and the uncovering of painful buried memories, Mary should receive part of the advance she was to be paid. This would later, when the book became published in 1998, cause much controversy over criminals profiting from their deeds. Mary thought and hoped that if she told her story, the media would leave her alone. Her hope for the book was to "set the record straight."

In *Cries Unheard*, one learns more of the appalling abuse Mary suffered as a child from her mother, Betty Bell. With Betty's repeated attempts at ridding herself of Mary failing, Betty found a use for Mary when she was four-years-old. She forced her daughter to take part in prostitution by pimping her to pedophiles. Sometimes Mary would be blindfolded, her mother would say it was a game, "blind man's bluff," and as Betty held Mary's head back with one hand twisted into her hair and with the other hand pinioned her arms behind her back allowed her clients to ejaculate into her mouth. Mary would promptly vomit when they had finished with her. On some occasions, the men would have anal sex with her and sometimes Betty whipped Mary for the entertainment of her clients.

Her mother told her that if she ever told anyone, she would be locked up forever and that no one would believe what she said anyway. After the sessions,

Betty would then reward Mary with treats and would treat her nicely for a bit, rather then shout, hit, and verbally abuse her, and Mary never told anyone until after her mother's death when she confessed, after much probing, to Gita Sereny.

What I find extraordinary is that before and during the trial and in the twelve years Mary was imprisoned, the system made no effort to understand the reasons for her offenses. The truth, uncovered by an author, only emerged thirty years after the offenses were committed.

The detective in charge of the investigation into the boys' murders, James Dobson, told Gitta Sereny,

"My function was to determine who had perpetrated the crime and how it was committed. In our system, it is not the business of the police to find out why crimes are committed. But as we have seen here, sadly, when the perpetrators are children, it doesn't appear that it is anyone's business."

To comprehend and explain Mary's crimes is not to justify or excuse her behavior. What she did was horrific and the suffering she caused Brian's and Martin's families horrendous.

Children who kill or maim need to be humanely detained for as long as they are a danger. But invariably children who kill are victims of extreme abuse themselves who, in my opinion, deserve compassion, not hysterical condemnation. In truth, how many of us can be sure that, with a childhood like Mary's, we wouldn't have done something equally depraved?

# Publication of *Cries Unheard*

When *Cries Unheard* was published in 1998, and it was learned that Mary had been paid £50,000 ($76,000) it infuriated the public, who still regarded Mary as a freak and evil monster, who was now profiting from her heinous crimes. The British tabloid headlines decried Mary Bell's "blood money" and "depraved story." Mary Bell was yet again branded as a monstrous incarnation of evil.

Even while the tabloids were denouncing Mary for taking money for a story that she had every right to tell, they were offering her far greater sums than she had been paid to cooperate with the book.

Tony Blair, then the British Prime Minister, publicly decried her pay. His home secretary, Jack Straw, criticized the payment to Mary in a published letter in the *British Sun* newspaper to the mothers of the murdered boys. He stated that Mary, by co-operating with the book, had forfeited her right to anonymity.

Within hours of the *Sun* newspaper publishing Jack Straw's condemnation of Mary, dozens of reporters descended on Mary's Victorian terraced house perched on a hillside in a south coast resort.

Mary was forced to phone the police who evacuated the family from their home where she had lived anonymously with her partner and 14-year-old daughter, with blankets over their heads to avoid the flash bulbs and shouts from the media. It was in this traumatic manner that Mary's 14-year-old daughter learned of her mother's past. They were taken into protective custody to a secret address.

Mary has since said that her daughter accepts her identity and forgives her and said to her,

"Mum, why didn't you tell me? You were just a kid, younger than I am now."

Gita Sereny, said that she paid Mary Bell because,

"If I hadn't done so, I would have made myself guilty of doing what has been done to her virtually since she was born: to USE her..."

Since Mary was released from prison, she has had three different identities and has had to move, after being identified, on at least five occasions. Mary, since her release, has led a law-abiding life and became a loving and caring mother to her straight-A student daughter when she could have very easily fallen into a life of repeated crime. She has succeeded in breaking the appalling cycle of abuse from which she as a child suffered.

But Mary lives with the guilt of her crimes and the suffering she caused every day of her life. A guilt she will never be free from, which is probably as it should be.

When Mary's daughter turned eighteen, the court order giving her and her daughter anonymity ran out. In May of 2003, Mary won a High Court case to have her own anonymity and that of her daughter extended for life.

In 2009, Mary Bell became a grandmother. The High Court order protecting her was updated to include Mary`s grandchild, who was referred to in court as 'Z.'

June Richardson, 64, whose four-year-old son Martin Brown was suffocated by Mary, on hearing the news of Mary's grandchild said,

*"I will never see a grandchild from my son. I hope every time she looks at this baby she realizes*

*what my family is missing out on because of what she has done."*

# SOURCES

Cries Unheard: Why Children Kill: The Story of Mary Bell by Gitta Sereny

Documentary; The Mary Bell Case. Blakeway Productions for the BBC

The Telegraph   09 Jan 2009

http://www.trutv.com/library/crime/notorious_murders/famous/bell/index_1.html

The Guardian. 30 April 1998

http://news.bbc.co.uk/2/hi/uk_news/3043567.stm

# OTHER BOOKS BY SYLVIA PERRINI

## MURDER IN THE FAMILY SERIES

TILL DEATH DO US PART: DEADLY DIVORCES. When marriage turns to murder.
STOLEN LIVES: TRUE CRIME: MOMS WHO KILLED THEIR KIDS
KILLER KIDS: PARRICIDE  Children Who Kill Their Parents
KILLER DADS: TRUE CRIME: DADS WHO KILLED THEIR KIDS: PATERNAL FILICIDE

## WOMEN SERIAL KILLERS SERIES

WOMEN SERIAL KILLERS OF THE 17th CENTURY (WOMEN WHO KILL)
ISBN-10: 1482657805

**ISBN-13:** 978-1482657807

This was the century when royal poison scandals sent shockwaves throughout Europe. The scandals so rocked France, that Louis XIV in 1662, passed a law stopping the sale of poisonous substances to people other than professionals, and for all purchasers to be registered. In this short booklet of approximately 9,300 words, best selling author Sylvia Perrini takes a look at some of the most prolific women poisoners of this century, and a look at one woman, who did not use poison, just torture. Be prepared to be shocked

## WOMEN MURDERERS OF THE 18th CENTURY (WOMEN WHO KILL)

**ISBN-10:**1482678640

**ISBN-13:**978-1482678642

Life in the 18th Century was a time of great change. It is often referred to as the Age of Enlightenment. Throughout Europe, more people were learning to read, and becoming interested in reason and science. By the end of the 18th century Science and Artistic academies had become well established all over Europe. But life for many was extremely hard. Women had little rights. Indeed, a judge in England stated that it was "perfectly legal for a man to beat his wife, as long as he used a stick no thicker than his thumb" Women were regarded as the weaker sex, emotionally and intellectually. Their job was to nurture their men and children, to be gentle and kind. In this short book best selling author Sylvia Perrini looks at several profiles of women in this era who shocked the societies in which they lived.

**WOMEN SERIAL KILLERS OF THE 19th CENTURY: The Golden Age Of Poisons (WOMEN WHO KILL)**

**ISBN-10:**148269672X

**ISBN-13:**978-1482696721

The 19th Century is frequently regarded as the heyday of the poisoner. In the beginning to the middle of the nineteenth century, a poisoning panic engrossed the public imagination. In the Times newspaper in England, between 1830 and 1839, fifty-nine cases of murder by poisoning were reported. By the 1840s, the number reported had risen to hundreds. And, of these hundreds of poisonings, sixty percent involved women murderers. In this fascinating book, best selling author Sylvia Perrini, looks at serial women killers around the world in the 19th Century. Nearly all the cases, but not all, involve poisoning. This book contains profiles of women mentioned in Women Serial Killers of the 19th Century Vol 1 and Women Serial killers of the 19th Century Vol 2. Both available as kindle books on Amazon.

**WOMEN SERIAL KILLERS OF THE**

# 20th CENTURY (WOMEN WHO KILL)
**ISBN-10:** 1483953963

**ISBN-13:** 978-1483953960

The 20th-century like the previous centuries has seen no end of murders by women with poison as their choice of weapon. And, like the previous centuries the murders have been just as cold and calculating. Why do women prefer to murder with poison? It avoids physical confrontation. It is cleaner than the ugly bloodied scenes of guns or knives. And they believe it is a method that will allow them to get away with murder. Those lucky few, who have managed to survive an attempted murder by these women, have described been poisoned as being equal to being devoured alive.

However, the 20th century has also seen murders committed by women with guns, and in the case of Dana Gray, with physical violence. Dana is a rarity among women serial killers, both in her choice of victim and her hands-on method of using her hands, a cord or rope, and an object in which to batter her victim. Aileen Wuornus, was described in the popular press as the first American woman serial killer. This is totally incorrect. American women serial killers existed long before Aileen Wuornos was born. So what leads a woman to commit serial murder?

The vast majority of serial murders committed by women in the 20th century, as in earlier centuries, have been committed for money and materialistic gain. Other reasons include a need to overpower, attention seeking behavior and personality disorders to name just a few. In this book, I examine the profiles of twenty-five women serial killers, all of whom acted alone. I have not included mother`s who kill their children, as I believe, that is a subject that deserves to be written about entirely separately. Welcome to the world of 20th century women serial killers.

## OR BUY THE ABOVE FOUR BOOKS IN ONE

### WOMEN SERIAL KILLERS THROUGH TIME (4 Books in 1)
**ISBN-10:** 1484044266
**ISBN-13:** 978-1484044261

### ANGELS OF DEATH; NURSES WHO KILL (WOMEN SERIAL KILLERS)
ISBN-10: 1501093096
ISBN-13: 978-1501093098

In this book, historian and bestselling author Sylvia Perrini looks at some cases of serial killers, all of whom were female nurses. The crimes of these nurses are heinous and shocking.

Luckily, nurses, who murder their patients, are the exception. They are not the rule. However, the number of cases of nurses accused and convicted of murdering patients is rising. It's almost enough to give you a phobia about going into hospital!!

## I DON'T LIKE MONDAYS: FEMALE RAMPAGE KILLERS (WOMEN WHO KILL)

**ISBN-10:** 1489533966

**ISBN-13:** 978-1489533968

"I DON'T LIKE MONDAYS."

The Famous hit song "I don't like Mondays" penned by Bob Geldof, was written after the school shootings in San Diego, California, committed by Brenda Spencer. Once she was apprehended and asked why she had done it. Her reply was:

"I don't like Mondays, do you?"

When one thinks of spree killers or rampage killers, normally one thinks of a male. Men such as the Aurora Colorado Movie Theater James Eagan Holmes, Seung-Hui Cho Virginia Tech Massacre, Columbine school killers Eric David Bennet and Dylan Bennet Klebold, Adam

Lanza at Sandy Hook Elementary School, and the 2011 massacre at a summer camp in Norway, by Anders Behring Breivik to name just a few.

Yet, women have also committed these crimes just not in such large numbers as men

### SUGAR N`SPICE: TEEN GIRLS WHO KILL (FEMALE KILLERS)

**ISBN-10:** 149045845X

**ISBN-13:** 978-1490458458

Murder is horrific whenever it happens and in what ever circumstances. But when a murder is carried out by a young girl, not much more than a child, it is doubly horrific.

What is it that goes wrong in the lives and minds of these girls that grow up to be teenage killers? Girls who ruthlessly murder strangers, young children, parents, and others?"

### BABY FARMERS OF THE 19th CENTURY (WOMEN WHO KILL)

**ISBN-10:** 1484128729

**ISBN-13:** 978-1484128725

The practice of baby farming came about in late Victorian times. In this era, there was a great social stigma attached to having a child out of marriage and no adequate contraception existed. In this period of time, no child protection services or regulated adoption agencies were in existence.

A number of untrained women offered adoption and fostering services to unmarried mothers who would hand over their baby and a cash payment. The mothers hoped that this payment would find stable, happy homes for their babies. And in the case of weekly payments that they would at some time in the future be able to re-claim their child.

It was, without doubt, one of the most sickening aspects of Victorian times, not only in Britain but also in its colonies as well.

Many of these fostering and adoption agencies were bona fide, but a frightening number were not. They became known as baby farms.

In this short book, bestselling author, Sylvia Perrini, introduces us to some of these baby farmers.

**SHE DEVILS OF AUSTRALIA**
**ISBN-13: 978-1497345911**

In Australia, one thinks that it is the dangerous animals and critters one needs to be afraid of, but what of the female human species?

Our society can barely account for evil in males, let alone imagine it in females. The female nests, creates, and nurtures doesn't she or is it that we just want to believe in the intrinsic non-threatening nature of women?

Violence is generally considered the territory of the male. People believe that violence is a masculine trait caused by the hormone testosterone. Men are seen as the cause of violence, and women and children the ones who suffer. Literature through the centuries abounds with the submissiveness of female flesh, its compliant form, its penetrability. The female body gives life itself. Women do not physically dominate, thrust, and swagger. Women create, while men destroy.

It is unfortunately a grave misconception to believe that the human female is not capable of violence, as the profiles in this book sadly demonstrate. In this book, author Sylvia Perrini looks at some of the worst murders committed by Australian women.

Welcome to the world of the Australian SHE DEVIL

For more books by Ms Perrini please visit her Amazon author page at
http://www.amazon.com/SYLVIA-PERRINI/e/B007WRWEI0/ref=ntt_athr_dp_pel_1

Printed in Great Britain
by Amazon